AEI LEGISLATIVE ANALYSES
Balanced analyses of current proposals before the Congress, prepared with the help of specialists in law, economics, and government

Limiting Presidential and Congressional Terms

1979

96th Congress
1st Session

AMERICAN ENTERPRISE INSTITUTE
*for Public Policy Research
Washington, D.C.*

JK
550
.A43

161631

ISBN 0-8447-0219-6
Legislative Analysis No. 4, 95th Congress
October 1979

Contents

1 Introduction 1

2 Historical Background 2
    The President: Length of Term and Total Tenure 2
    The Congress: Lengths of Terms and Total Tenure 5

**3 Current Proposals for Altering Terms
or Limiting Tenure** 10
    Limiting Presidents to a Single Term 10
    Limiting House and Senate Tenure 18

    Notes to Text 30

1
INTRODUCTION

> I have begun to realize lately that if I could just, by the stroke of the pen, change the Constitution, I think one six-year term would be preferable. The reason is that no matter what I do as President now, where I am really trying to ignore politics and stay away from any sort of campaign plans and so forth, a lot of the things I do are colored through the news media and in the minds of the American people by, "Is this a campaign ploy or is it genuinely done in the best interest of our country without any sort of personal advantage involved?"
>
> I think that if I had a six-year term, without any prospect of reelection, it would be an improvement. . . . I have come to that conclusion reluctantly.[1]

This statement by President Jimmy Carter illustrates one of the many issues associated with limiting the terms of elected officials. The president would like to be free to make decisions without having to concern himself with reelection, assuming that such a condition would reduce criticism. It is not at all unusual for a president to propose structural change of this kind when faced with the frustrations of leadership. It is the case, however, that a seemingly simple reform—for example, altering the permissible length of public service—seldom is as uncomplicated as advertised. Such reforms often grow out of fundamental views about democracy, typically extending to representation, responsiveness, accountability, and effectiveness in the job.

President Carter believes that he can accomplish his objectives and serve the public interest by being more detached from electoral politics. Others characterize his conclusions as being fundamentally antidemocratic—that is, indicating the wish to exercise power without being accountable to the people through elections.

Proposals to limit congressional service have also been offered in recent years. The basic issues differ somewhat from those associated with limiting presidential terms, as do the causes that give rise to the proposals. One of the differences is related to the prominent status of the president as compared with that of members of Congress. Certain observers believe, however, that in both cases the public interest is better served by relatively high turnover. To these observers, the advantages of stability do not outweigh the disadvantages and temptations of tenure. This legislative analysis will canvass reasons for the establishment of the present terms of office and will also explore arguments for limiting tenure at this juncture in history.

2
Historical Background

The President: Length of Term and Total Tenure

The Constitutional Plan. Article II, Section 1, of the Constitution states simply: "The executive power shall be vested in a President of the United States of America. He shall hold his office during the term of four years." No mention is made of how many terms might be served, though that subject was discussed during the formation of the Constitution. The delegates to the convention moved back and forth several times with regard to both the length of the presidential term of office and the total tenure, and these issues were associated with other issues in the minds of the delegates. At first there was agreement on a single seven-year term; later a renewable seven-year term was approved. Then a renewable six-year term was agreed to; this was followed by approval once again of a single seven-year term and, finally, by agreement on a renewable four-year term. Other proposals were made for single eight-, eleven-, fifteen-, and twenty-year terms, and for no more than six years' service in twelve, and for service "during good behavior." (See Table 1 for the chronology and for details of the various proposals.)

In part, this variation was related to the method by which the president was to be chosen. Consistently sensitive to the need for the separation and balance of powers, many delegates believed that if the president were to be selected by Congress then only a single term should be permitted. It was feared that renewable terms might lead to congressional control or domination of the executive.

On the other hand, concern was expressed that a single term might "destroy the great motive to good behavior, the hope of being rewarded by a reappointment." In reporting Gouverneur Morris's remarks on this subject, Madison wrote: "It was saying to him, make hay while the sun shines."[2]

As might be expected, Madison was especially protective of the separation of powers and thus eventually was supportive of a more independent election.

> If it be essential to the preservation of liberty that the Legis: Execut: & Judiciary powers be separate, it is essential to a maintenance of the separation, that they should be independent of each other. The Executive could not be independent of the Legislature [sic], if dependent on the pleasure of that branch for reappointment.[3]

The renewable four-year term, with selection by the electoral college, was developed in the so-called Committee of Eleven, of which Madison was a member. The committee report provided that the Senate would select the president if two or more candidates tied or if no one received a majority. Since it was judged by some that "nineteen times out of twenty the President would be chosen by the Senate,"[4] this proposal was viewed as little improvement over selection by Congress in the first place.

On September 6, 1787, Roger Sherman of Connecticut resolved the matter by essentially making the House of Representatives responsible for this one function. The House would choose the president in the case of a tie or when no one candidate received a majority, but for this single purpose each state would be equal as in the Senate. Regardless how many representatives it might have, each state would have only one vote for president. The Senate was to choose the vice-president in case of a tie. Colonel George Mason of Virginia "liked the latter mode best as lessening the aristocratic influence of the Senate,"[5] and it passed by a vote of ten to one.

Concern over the likelihood that the legislature would select the president proved to be misplaced, particularly after the passage of the Twelfth Amendment. This amendment was adopted to avoid a repetition of the situation that had occurred with the election of 1800 in which Thomas Jefferson and Aaron Burr had received equal votes in the electoral college. The final decision was thus thrown into the House of Representatives, despite the electors' intention that Jefferson be president and Burr vice-president.

The difference between the procedure defined by the Twelfth Amendment and that laid down originally is in the provision the amendment makes for a separate designation by the electors of their choices for president and vice-president. With the popular election of the electoral college, the president gained even greater distance and independence from the legislature.

In summary, the founders wanted to limit the president's term to maintain the separation of powers, not to permit freedom from political accountability. The arrangements they provided, plus the clarifications in the Twelfth Amendment and the eventual emergence of the two-party system, resolved the issue in favor of an independent executive.

Subsequent Proposals and Changes. The issue of limited terms did not die.[6] Instead, other fears developed—ironically, most of them associated with the power of an independent executive. Although, with his popularity, he might have been expected to serve several terms, George Washington was reluctant to seek even a second term. Madison, Hamilton, and Jefferson all urged him to reconsider, and he was reelected unanimously by the electoral college. As the end of Washington's second term approached, the Federalists were concerned about succession.

> "If a storm gather," Hamilton asked Washington, "how can you retreat?" Washington wrote firmly that he would "close my public life on March 4, 1797, after which no consideration under heaven that I can foresee shall again draw me from the walks of private life."[7]

Washington was determined this time, announcing in his farewell address: "I should now apprise you of the resolution I have formed to decline being considered among the number of those out of whom a choice is to be made." Thus, an important precedent was established by the then aging president—a precedent followed by all presidents up to Grant, who in 1875 made it clear that he would favor a third term. The House passed a resolution asserting that the Washington precedent had become "a part of our republican system of government, and that any departure from this time-honored custom would be unwise, unpatriotic, and fraught with peril to our free institutions."[8] The resolution was supported by a large majority of Democrats *and* Republicans, which clearly suggested that Grant could not secure the Republican nomination.[9]

Another Republican did, in fact, seek more than eight years as president (even though his election would not be considered a third term under the Twenty-second Amendment of March 1, 1951). Theodore Roosevelt served as president from September 1901 to March 1909, first filling out McKinley's term, then being elected in his own right. Before the 1908 election, Roosevelt declared support for the two-term limit. In 1912, however, he ran as a candidate on the Progressive party ticket, declaring that

> if at some time he had declined "a third cup of coffee" nobody would suppose that he had meant never to take another cup. "I meant, of course," said he, "a third consecutive term."[10]

Although there were indications that, had he been healthy, Woodrow Wilson would have sought a third term in 1920,[11] it remained for another Roosevelt to violate Washington's precedent. Franklin D. Roosevelt was overwhelmingly reelected in 1940 and then again in 1944.

Nearly 360 proposals have been introduced through the years to alter the president's term in some manner. Over half of these proposals have been for a six-year term, and half of the six-year term proposals have included the single-term limitation. A change in the number of terms of office for a president did not occur until Franklin D. Roosevelt departed from Washington's precedent. Several proposals, most of them for two four-year terms, were introduced between 1940 and 1947, but it was not until the Republicans gained a majority in both houses of Congress in the 1946 elections that an amendment was approved by Congress and submitted to the states for ratification. In the Eightieth Congress both the single six-year term and two four-year terms were given serious consideration. The sponsor of the six-year-term proposal, Representative Everett M. Dirksen (R-Ill.), relied on very much the same rationale that President Carter relied on over thirty years later—that is, that "all bargaining and compromise frequently resorted to with hope of re-election would be eliminated."[12] Others concurred with this view. Still it was the two-term limitation that received majority support in the House Committee on the Judiciary and that was passed on the floor by a vote of 285 to 121. The Senate Committee on the Judiciary reported an amended version of H.J. Res. 27, including a provision to send the amendment to state conventions instead of state legislatures for ratification. Amendments were introduced on the Senate floor to restore the House version, and the resolution was passed by a vote of 59 to 23. Unsuccessful attempts were made in both houses to substitute the single six-year term for the two-term limitation.

The Twenty-second Amendment to the Constitution was ratified March 1, 1951. It contains the following provision:

> No person shall be elected to the office of the President more than twice, and no person who has held the office of President, or acted as President, for more than two years of a term to which some other person was elected President shall be elected to the office of the President more than once.

Effectively, then, a president could serve for nearly ten years if assuming office because of the death, incapacity, or resignation of an incumbent. Or a president could serve two full terms as a consequence of election. Or a president might be limited to just one elected term, as Gerald Ford was because he assumed the Presidency before the midpoint of Richard Nixon's second term. Thus the range of eligibility is from six years plus one day to ten years minus one day.[13]

While the passage of the Twenty-second Amendment quieted the demand for change for a time, the 1970s witnessed renewed interest in the subject. With a two-term limitation in place, attention turned to the single six-year term.

THE CONGRESS: LENGTHS OF TERMS AND TOTAL TENURE

The Lengths of Terms Set in the Constitution. The Articles of Confederation provided for a unicameral legislature with delegates appointed annually by the state legislatures. A state was permitted to appoint from two to seven delegates, but each state had only one vote "in determining questions." As if annual appointment were not in itself a sufficient check, state legislatures were empowered to recall delegates at any time and to "send others in their stead," and delegates were limited in service to "three years in any term of six years." Edmund Cody Burnett, in his careful examination of the Continental Congress, observed: "By this measure Congress effectively innoculated itself with the germ of pernicious anemia."[14]

Having opted for the untested virtues of turnover as a protection against the presumed evils of continuity, the Congress proceeded in 1784 "to make an inventory of its present stock of members to determine whether there were any violations of that constitutional provision, whether any members were tarrying beyond their appointed terms."[15]

An investigation committee found that Samuel Osgood of Massachusetts was, indeed, serving beyond his three years in six. Osgood withdrew, "vociferating the while (although with reservations) a 'farewell all Connection with public life!'; he was 'inexpressibly disgusted with it.'"[16] The committee also determined that two Delaware delegates were not eligible to serve after February 1, and that two Rhode Island delegates must leave in May. The Delaware delegates did not dispute their ouster, but the gentlemen from Rhode Island did. The debate that ensued was bitter.

Samuel Hardy of Virginia asserted that the dispute had given rise to "more altercation" than he had ever seen, either in Congress or in any other place, while Monroe declared, "I never saw more indecent conduct in any assembly before." Before the case could be brought to decision it began to appear that, if the Rhode Island delegates should be ousted, Congress would practically be stopped from further business; accordingly, the matter was dropped.[17]

This background is important primarily because it provides a context for the debate on legislative terms at the Constitutional Convention. The Continental Congress was well represented in Philadelphia: thirty-two of the thirty-nine signers of the Constitution had served as congressional delegates, as had several who attended but did not sign. It is not surprising, therefore, that the one-year term received serious consideration for the House of Representatives and that limitation of terms received almost no attention. Left blank in the Virginia Plan, the initial proposals for length of the House term were for one, two, and three years, with most attention and support given to one or three years. Elbridge Gerry of Massachusetts stated the case for one year: "The people of New England will never give up the point of annual elections." He considered annual elections as the only defense of the people against tyranny. He was as much against a triennial House as against a hereditary executive.[18]

Madison argued the case for three years in the following words:

> Instability is one of the great vices of our republics, to be remedied. Three years will be necessary, in a Government so extensive, for members to form any knowledge of the various interests of the States to which they do not belong, and of which they can know but little from the situation and affairs of their own. One year will be almost consumed in preparing for and travelling to and from the seat of national business.[19]

It is interesting to note that, at least as Madison recorded the debate, no mention was made either of limiting total tenure or of the need to make terms coincident with those of either the president or senators.

The compromise on the length of the House term was introduced on June 21, 1787, by Edmund Randolph of Virginia, who moved to substitute two years for three. Several other delegates addressed the question, but perhaps the issue was best joined in the statements of Roger Sherman of Connecticut and Alexander Hamilton of New York. Sherman argued that "the Representatives ought to return home and mix with the people" so that they might not "acquire the habits of the [seat of government] which might differ from those of their Constituents." Hamilton pointed out that "frequency of elections tended to make the people listless to them; and to facilitate the success of little cabals."[20]

It seems likely that once the two-year term was arrived at as a compromise on the length of the House term, the question of further control through limiting total tenure did not arise: that is, the one-year-term advocates were willing to accept two years as retaining the advantages of frequency, while the three-year term advocates were willing to accede to the compromise (if somewhat more reluctantly) as incorporating greater continuity and stability.

Debate on the issue of limiting total tenure for senators might have been expected, in view of the general acceptance of relatively long terms for senators. But it did not come (at least it was not recorded in Madison's notes). Instead, the debate centered on the duration of the term, with some delegates advocating as little as four years (with one-fourth elected each year) and others urging that a senator hold office "during good behavior." Clearly, all delegates viewed the Senate as quite a different legislative body from the House. Even those supporting the shorter terms accepted the concept of the Senate as providing greater continuity and stability. The debate then focused on how this goal might be achieved. For Madison and his supporters the ideal Senate would be populated by those attentive to the possible excesses of republican government.

> In framing a system which we wish to last for ages, we should not lose sight of the changes which ages will produce. An increase of population will of necessity increase the proportion of those who will labour under all the hardships of life, and secretly sigh for a more equal distribution of its blessings. These may in time outnumber those who are placed above the feelings of indigence. According to the equal laws of suffrage, the power will slide into the hands of the former. . . . symptoms [sic] of a leveling spirit, . . . have sufficiently appeared in certain quarters to give notice of the future danger. How is this danger to be guarded against on republican principles? How is the danger in all cases of interested coalitions to oppress the minority to be guarded against?[21]

Madison's response was that a second legislative body "sufficiently respectable for its wisdom and virtue" might well curb the tendencies referred to but only if its members were given "a considerable duration." Hamilton agreed.

Roger Sherman believed that good behavior was guaranteed only with frequent elections. By implication he suggested that tenure during good behavior lacked proper enforcement.

> Government is instituted for those who live under it. It ought therefore to be so constituted as not to be dangerous to their liberties. . . . Frequent elections are necessary to preserve the good behavior of rulers. They also tend to give permanency to the Government, by preserving that good behavior, because it ensures their re-election.[22]

Terms of five, six, seven, and nine years were debated by the delegates before they finally compromised on a term of six years. The six-year compromise provided a two-year check in that one-third of the Senate would go out every second year. The provisions of this compromise prevented the limiting of total service from becoming a major issue. For advocates of a short term, the six-year term with one-third turnover every two years ensured frequency of state legislative involvement in appointment. And advocates of a life term obviously were not persuaded to limit terms. Thus, the political-accountability issue was resolved for most delegates with the frequency of election or appointment for both houses, and the issue of citizen representatives developing legislative careers was not recognized or discussed.

The entire question of legislative terms was not as painful for the delegates as was the question of a presidential term. The issue was settled relatively early—in June—for both the House and the Senate. The reason is simple: the presidential term was inexorably linked to the manner of selection. Since the latter was unsettled until the last, the matter of term length and limitation for the presidency was reopened frequently.

Earlier Proposals for Change. The Constitution has remained unchanged in regard to House and Senate terms, though changes have been proposed from time to time (particularly for House terms). Only the Seventeenth Amendment ratified April 4, 1913, directly affected the selection and status of national legislators. The six-year Senate term was reiterated and popular election was substituted for choice by state legislatures.

Very few changes were proposed in the first hundred years. Turnover was high among members of the House and thus the question of limiting total tenure, in particular, did not arise. Throughout most of the nineteenth century service in the House was likely to be a matter of one or, at most, a few terms. Turnover of House membership ranged from 30 percent to over 60 percent at *every* election, and the average number of terms of previous service represented by a new House generally ranged from one (or even less) to one-and-a-half terms.[23]

With the emergence of House service as a career, proposals were introduced to extend the term of service—most frequently to four years. Seldom did these proposals receive serious attention, however. In 1906 a proposal for the popular election of senators, which included a four-year term for House members, was voted on in the House but failed to receive the required two-thirds majority. An attempt was again made in 1931 to include a four-year-term provision in the Twentieth Amendment—once more without success. The proposal has also come up from time to time in connection with other reform efforts, and Presidents Truman, Eisenhower, and Johnson also suggested the change. President Johnson actually mentioned it in his 1966 State of the Union Message, following up with a specific proposal that House members be elected in presidential election years. In 1965 the Joint Committee on the Organization of Congress frequently discussed the four-year term with witnesses during its hearings, and Subcommittee No. 5 of the House Committee on the Judiciary held hearings specifically on the proposed change. In 1966, after President Johnson's proposal was introduced, the Subcommittee on Constitutional Amendments of the Senate Committee on the Judiciary also held hearings.[24]

A number of polls were taken during 1965–1966 to measure both congressional and public interest in the four-year-term proposal. A strong House supporter, Frank Chelf (D-Ky.), polled both House and Senate members on his proposal to elect half of the House in presidential years and the other half at midterm. The House results were 254 in favor, 41 opposed, and 67 in doubt. His Senate poll revealed that "two-thirds of that body are for this bill." A poll taken by the *Congressional Quarterly* after the President's speech in 1966 found less support. Members were asked simply: "Do you favor a four-year House term?" Less than half responded (251 of 535), and the split was 55 percent in favor, 45 percent opposed. The Gallup Poll showed public support for the change to be growing, with 40 percent in favor in 1946, 51 percent in 1961, and 61 percent in 1966.[25]

A poll taken by the Brookings Institution in connection with a study of the four-year-term proposals found less support than did earlier polls. Administered in 1966, the Brookings poll distinguished among the various proposals for change, namely: a four-year term concurrent with the president's term, a four-year term with all members elected at midterm, a four-year term with half of the members elected every two years, and a three-year term. It became apparent with this poll that no one proposal had the support of a majority. The president's proposal for the election of House members in presidential election years was opposed by 77.9 percent of the 318 House respondents. Only the staggered elections proposal had sizable support (46.7 percent in favor, 46.8 percent opposed, 6.5 percent neutral). Maintenance of the two-year term had the support of 61.4 percent of the respondents. Previous polls had erred (1) in not distinguishing among the various proposals, and (2) in not asking for members' views on the two-year term. The Brookings poll showed that those who favored one proposal strongly disapproved of others.[26]

Most proposals to limit the number of congressional terms are of rather recent vintage; three-fourths of the proposals since 1789 have been introduced since 1970. Interest in term limitation appears to coincide with recent concerns about the advantage enjoyed by incumbents. Typically, over 90 percent of House members who seek reelection are returned to office. Those who value turnover are disturbed by this development and have, therefore, proposed that members be permitted to serve no longer than a set number of years. Thus, we observe two developments: (1) interest in lengthening terms with the growth of a more professional, career-oriented House of Representatives, and (2) interest in limiting service with the realization of incumbency advantage and lower membership turnover.

Historically, Senate terms have not been the subject of as many proposals for change as have House terms. Amendments to set Senate service at one eight-year term were introduced in 1896, 1904, and 1906, but these efforts received no attention. Twelve other resolutions were introduced before 1970 to limit Senate service to one, two, or three six-year terms. Hearings were actually held on a one-term limit in the Seventy-ninth Congress, and Senator W. Lee O'Daniel (D-Tex.) introduced an amendment to the proposed Twenty-second Amendment to limit all elected officials in the national government to a single six-year term. But the greatest amount of activity in limiting congressional service has occurred in the 1970s, particularly since 1975.[27]

3

CURRENT PROPOSALS FOR ALTERING TERMS OR LIMITING TENURE

Most recent presidential-term amendments have proposed a single six-year term. The Twenty-second Amendment had the effect of narrowing the subject of debate. Under recent proposals, a vice-president who assumes the presidency typically is permitted to run for a full term as president only if he or she has served fewer than three full years as president. Thus, the conceivable range of eligibility for a president popularly elected would be from six years to nine years minus one day. One proposal, introduced in 1979 by Elwood Hillis (R-Ind.), did provide for two six-year terms, with a vice-president eligible for election to just one six-year term if he or she had served more than three years as president. In this case the range of eligibility for a president able to win reelection would be from nine years plus one day to fifteen years minus one day.

A variety of proposals has been offered for limiting congressional service. Changes in length of term and limits on the number of terms are combined for House terms. The most popular change in length is, of course, to four years. A twelve-year overall limitation is most often proposed—six two-year terms, four three-year terms, or three four-year terms.

Those proposing a change in length of term are faced with the problem of determining when the members should run—that is, with the president, during the midterm, or one-half in each election. The 1979 resolutions provide either concurrent election with the president or staggered elections. Thus, the same disagreements characterizing the debate in 1966 may be expected to come to the surface again.

Most of the Senate term limitations are for two terms or twelve years. Only one proposal in recent years advocates lengthening the Senate term. A representative sample of the proposals offered in 1979 is summarized in Table 2.

LIMITING PRESIDENTS TO A SINGLE TERM

The rationale for (and thus the argument against) further limiting the president's term is different from that for limiting congressional terms. For the most part, those favoring the single six-year term see it as a way of freeing the president from partisan politics. Those favoring a cap on congressional terms, on the other hand, are worried chiefly about incumbency advantage in elections and the power of members in Washington. These differences justify separate treatment for the executive and legislative branches.

Frequent reference is made by proponents of a single presidential term to the proposal for a single seven-year term that had the early approval of the delegates to the Constitutional Convention in Philadelphia. Therefore, it is worth reiterating that this provision was associated with congressional selection of the president. Political accountability to an electorate was not considered one way or the other, because at no time was popular election seriously entertained.

Views of Supporters of a Single Term. Generally, the rhetoric supporting the single six-year-term can be divided into (1) a general view of politics that leads to support for change, (2) estimates of the length of time likely to be required to achieve desired goals, and (3) a set of expectations regarding critical presidential relationships (for example, with Congress, the bureaucracy, the public, the parties) and personal behavior.[28]

Social and political reforms, when probed, typically reveal broader opinions on government and society. The single six-year-term proposal is no exception. Its proponents are willing to support election as a method of selecting a president, but they do not feel very confident that reelection is, in Gouverneur Morris's words, "the great motive to good behavior." In fact, they believe the opposite. Seeking reelection, in their view, is likely to lead a president toward favoring special interests and away from serving the public interest. In fact, the general rhetoric is not unlike that supporting the trustee concept over the delegate concept of representation (that is, a representative bound to offer his or her best judgment, not one bound to estimating the wants and needs of electoral groups). Perhaps the classic statement on this subject was that offered by Andrew Jackson in 1830:

> In order, particularly, that his appointment may as far as possible be placed beyond the reach of any improper influences; in order that he may approach the solemn responsibilities of the highest office in the gift of a free people uncommitted to any other course than the strict line of constitutional duty, and that the securities of this independence may be rendered as strong as the nature of power and the weakness of its possessor will admit, I cannot too earnestly invite your attention to the propriety of promoting such an amendment of the Constitution as will render him ineligible after one term of service.[29]

Milton Eisenhower, brother of Dwight Eisenhower and president of Johns Hopkins University, argues, "If there were evils in permitting the president to run for a third term—as the Congress and states decided—those same evils apply to election for a second term."[30]

For Jackson, limited service also offered the advantage of ensuring turnover. In line with his republican principles, Jackson believed that power corrupts and that all citizens have a right to positions of influence.

> There are, perhaps, few men who can for any great length of time enjoy office and power without being more or less under the influence of feelings unfavorable to the faithful discharge of their public duties. . . . More is lost by the long continuance of men in office than is generally to

> be gained by their experience. . . . In a country where offices are created solely for the benefit of the people no one man has any more intrinsic right to official station than another. . . . The proposed limitation . . . would, by prompting that rotation which constitutes a leading principle in the republican creed, give healthful action to the system.[31]

Here, then, is a general picture of politics as it applies to the presidency. Although not all proponents so clearly articulate their premises, many appear to be driven by one or more aspects of Jackson's argument. These premises may show up as the frustrations of incumbent presidents—as with the statement of President Carter quoted at the opening of this analysis—or as the personal preferences of publicists who believe that politics interferes with, rather than facilitates, realization of the public interest. As Griffin Bell, Carter's attorney general, has stated: "The single six-year term would permit the long-term, steady planning and implementation that our government needs, plus saving that fourth year now lost to campaigning."[32]

If reelection is more a hindrance than a help, the question becomes one of estimating the proper length of the term of office. Andrew Jackson proposed a four- or six-year term. Senator John D. Works (R-Calif.), author in 1912 of a proposal for a single six-year term, argued that the length of term was less significant than the ineligibility for reelection.

> I am not wedded to any particular term for the President, long or short, as I have said the length of term is not the important matter to be considered. It is the right of the President under the present rule to succeed himself that I am combating.
>
> I would have no objection to four years or eight years as the term of office. I would not be willing to go beyond eight years.[33]

Earlier in his remarks, however, Senator Works had noted that he "would rather—much rather—see one term of ten years than two terms of four years each in immediate succession."

The six-year term is justified in today's government as a reasonable compromise between four years and eight years. Four years is estimated to be too short a term in view of the complexities of the modern presidency. Eight years is judged to be too long to wait should the president not be fulfilling the responsibilities of the office. It is important to mention that little or no systematic analysis is offered in support of the six-year compromise. The rationale is typically of the sort just cited (that is, it is an individual's best guess as to the length of service that may suit the purposes intended). Thus, for example, one finds no systematic examination of the experience in those states with single-term executives, or of the reasoning that led many of them to abandon the practice.[34]

An entire range of expectations follows from this supporting rationale for a single six-year term.

Effect on relations with particular groups. First, there are expectations regarding the critical relationships between the president and various institutions or groups with which he must deal.

1. Congress: The relationships with Congress, it is argued, will be less subject to conflict and rivalry. The president will be free to shape his congressional program to suit his concept of what is best for the public interest rather than attempting to suit every special interest. The presidential record will be less tested in congressional elections since the president will not be eligible for reelection. Congress will respect the presidency as a source of comprehensive and objective analysis of public problems. The president will consult with congressional leaders in the development of his program rather than relying heavily on personal advisers who are appointed primarily to ensure reelection. The media will support this orientation toward the public interest and will put pressure on Congress to work with the president.

2. The bureaucracy: The president, it is argued, will use bureaucratic expertise to greater advantage in the shaping of programs, since political pressures will be lessened. Presidential appointees will be in a much stronger position within the departments and agencies, as they will be free to concentrate on management rather than on the politics associated with reelecting the president.[35] The president, when free of political pressures, will also be free to select professionally qualified persons to these posts. And the appointees will have a longer period in which to take charge of the department or agency. Bureaucrats will perform more effectively because of the continuity of appointments and of programmatic direction.

3. The media: The relationship between the president and the media will be improved. The suspicion on the part of the press that every presidential action is taken to improve the president's chances of reelection will disappear, and reporters will concentrate on the president's efforts to solve public problems.[36] The president will be able to be more open with the press, thus relationships will be of greater benefit to public communication.

4. Special interest groups: The president will better serve special interests in the long run by weighing their demands against the broader public interest. Some claim that this will lead special interests to judge the overall effects of their demands. There will be fewer direct connections between interest groups and executive agencies, it is argued, since the appointments to those agencies will be more professional than political.

5. The political party: The president will not be committed to deal with the manifold electoral problems faced by the national, state, and local political parties. The parties, in turn, will be able to organize their fundraising and campaigning activities without the dominance of a presidential reelection bid. Political party leaders will be free to do what is best for their party instead of being constrained by the president's program and record. Closer relationships between party leaders in Congress and national and state organizations will be fostered as a consequence of the president's greater freedom from party obligations.

6. The general public: Above all, the president will be able to concentrate on an objective analysis of which programs are in the best interests of the nation as a whole. If reelection is not possible, the president will not be tempted to favor one special group over others. The dominant motive will be that of doing the best possible job rather than estimating which group will provide the greatest support.

This motivation at the highest levels may also influence the behavior of other elected officials and, acting in the broader public interest, may become a more general habit.

Other arguments for limiting the president's term in office. Other expectations or proponents are identified with the personal demands of the office.

1. The job takes its toll: An individual can no longer endure the stresses and strains of the presidency for eight years, particularly when there is also the need to seek reelection. Effectiveness is reduced, and presidents suffer mental anguish and physical debilitation. The single six-year term will reduce the strain by limiting the period of service. It may also have the effect of producing a more spirited approach to the job.

2. Seeking reelection is degrading: Senator Works was particularly distressed by this aspect of the presidency:

> [The president] goes out on the stump and discusses political questions, abuses his opponents, and urges the continuance in power of his party, involving his own reelection. To me it is a pitiful and humiliating spectacle.[37]

President Carter's statement cited earlier suggests that he may agree with this evaluation. By eliminating the need for this "spectacle," the single six-year term may be expected to elevate the reputation of the office of the presidency—a much needed development. John Connally argues:

> Nothing . . . would be more conducive to the restoration of the confidence of the people in our form of government . . . than the knowledge that an American President from the day of the assumption of office has fulfilled his political role and has no further except as the historians view him as a statesman.[38]

3. The president's family is in the public eye: The "dawn-to-dawn" media coverage of the president's immediate and extended family is unfair and unnecessary. It is also a consequence of reelection, since a president cannot afford to ignore the media in the first term, and the habit of coverage is established by the second term. With the single six-year term, a president will be in a position to protect both family and personal privacy.

Views of Opponents of a Single Term. Opponents of the single six-year term reject the general philosophy espoused by proponents and discount the probability and desirability of realizing many of the supposed benefits of the single term. They also have different views on the number of years to be served and, indeed, on the need for any limit at all.

Major reasons for opposition. Perhaps the most elegant statement of theory on the subject of term limitation was made by Alexander Hamilton in No. 72 of *The Federalist*. Hamilton identified many ill-effects of ineligibility:

> [It would result in] a diminution of the inducement to good behavior. . . . the temptation to sordid views, to peculation, . . . to usurpation.
>
> [It would result in] depriving the community of the advantage of the experience gained by the chief magistrate in the exercise of his office.
> . . .
> [It would lead to] banishing men from stations in which, in certain emergencies of state, their presence might be of the greatest moment.
> . . .
> . . . It would operate as a constitutional interdiction of stability in the administration.[39]

On balance, Hamilton was convinced that the president's term had to be of sufficient length and that reeligibility was essential.

> The first is necessary to give to the officer himself the inclination and the resolution to act his part well, and to the community time and leisure to observe the tendency of his measures, and thence to form an experimental estimate of their merits. The last is necessary to enable the people, when they see reason to approve of his conduct, to continue him in his station, in order to prolong the utility of his talents and virtues, and to secure to the government the advantage of permanency in a wise system of administration.[40]

Contemporary opponents of the six-year term argue that elections are the mainstay of responsible government. The public can and must be trusted to judge the performance of elected leaders. They argue that the one-term reform would be an infringement upon the people's right to vote for anyone they want to vote for, as many times as they want to vote.[41] Presidential power comes from elections and is maintained by presidential attentiveness to future elections. It is argued that if it were true that liberation from concern about reelection were the key to presidential statesmanship, then far greater achievements would occur during the second rather than the first terms of presidents, but this has not been the case. If campaigns and elections are faulty in some respects, they should be repaired, not abandoned.

Far from supporting a single six-year term, most of the persons in this group favor repealing the Twenty-second Amendment. It would be difficult, if not impossible, according to the opponents, to maintain democracy if the principal executive decision maker is removed from the political arena. Among its other effects, ineligibility would, and probably should, reduce the effectiveness of the president. Former President Harry S. Truman spoke with typical candor on the subject:

> You do not have to be very smart to know that an office-holder who is not eligible for reelection loses a lot of influence. So what have you done? You have taken a man and put him in the hardest job in the world, and sent him out to fight our battles in a life-and-death struggle—and you have sent him out to fight with one hand tied behind his back, because everyone knows he cannot run for reelection. . . .
>
> If he is not a good President, and you do not want to keep him, you do

not have to reelect him. There is a way to get rid of him and it does not require a constitutional amendment to do it.[42]

Here is a classic statement of the electoral accountability argument on the question of presidential terms. The president draws strength from election and the potential for reelection and should be held accountable at the polls for how he uses that strength. As columnist David S. Broder has stated:

> By arbitrarily lopping twenty-four months off his maximum term of service, it would limit his capacity to move policy in a sustained direction. . . . The proposal would also eliminate the use of the reelection campaign as a source of discipline on the exercise of presidential authority.[43]

On the subject of the presumed advantage of rotation in office, the opponents of term limitation argue, just as Hamilton argued, that the people should have a right to reelect a president for as long a period as that president serves well. Furthermore, a term limitation may force a president out at a particularly crucial time—for example, during wartime, economic depression, or a social or political crisis. These views are a natural extension of the emphasis on elections as the effective means for selecting and controlling political leaders.

Opponents are not persuaded that six years represents a rational term length. It may be too long if the president is ineffective; it may be too short if the opposite is true (or if an emergency arises just at the end of the term). George E. Reedy bluntly stated that the single six-year term provides "about two years of enthusiasm, two years of acquiescence, and two years of obstruction."[44] The advantage of the original constitutional design on this issue (that is, before ratification of the Twenty-second Amendment) was that it permitted a judgment to be made by the president and the public every four years. The two-term limitation changed that arrangement rather dramatically.

The estimation that six years is a proper term length is also subject to the objection that public problems and governmental organization may become still more complex in the future. At one time single-term advocates might well have supported a four-year presidency. Today it is estimated that six years is required. Perhaps seven or eight years will be reasonable by the year 2000. The writing of such temporal limitations into the Constitution holds risks. Again, the four-year term with eligibility for reelection provides greater flexibility for the future.

The opponents are also prepared to counter the entire range of expectations about the president's critical relationships with others and about the more personal effects of the office. Many of the objections to the claims of the proponents of the single term are based on grave doubts about the image of an unbiased president rising above politics to further the public interest. The opponents can be said to question whether such performance is possible or, if possible, is desirable. George E. Reedy states the case in the following words:

> The proposal for a six-year term is particularly interesting because it is based on the belief that a president's authority is somehow separable

from his political leadership. . . .
> The reality is quite different. A president whose political leadership is unchallenged can do just about anything. . . . A president whose political leadership has suffered from erosion is virtually helpless.[45]

This perspective shows up time and again in the rebuttals to proponents' arguments.

Adverse effect on relations with various groups. 1. Congress: The competitiveness characterizing presidential/congressional relations is in itself in the public interest. Each institution bears a separate relationship to the electorate, often producing different policy perspectives. Because there is no one "true" solution to public problems, this diversity is an advantage. But even if less rivalry is judged to be an advantage, it would not necessarily follow that a single six-year term would harmonize presidential/congressional relations. Thus, for example, a president elected by a minority of the popular vote in a bitter three-way contest would not necessarily draw strength from being ineligible for a second term. The conflicts inherent in the election itself may well carry over to presidential/congressional relations. In addition, Congress is unlikely to view the president as having some special advantage in formulating programs just because of that president's ineligibility for a second term. Members may be especially attentive because of the particular personal competencies of the incumbent, but this advantage would accrue to such a person regardless of length of term or eligibility for reelection. Finally, a president's record should be tested in all national elections. Such tests are potentially advantageous to the president and Congress for the learning process that takes place. David Broder argues that, "by taking him off the ballot in all congressional elections held during his tenure in office, it would reduce his influence with the legislative branch and make him even less able to resist the encroachment of Congress on his prerogatives."[46]

2. The bureaucracy: It is illusory to think that either a president ineligible for a second term or the heads of the departments and agencies will be free from political pressures. Those in positions of authority will, and should, be subject to political pressures in a democratic system of government. Political pressures help to determine purpose and thus should not be excluded from the White House. A purposeful president with the capacity to manage and direct political pressures who develops a coherent program, in cooperation with his advisers, will use the bureaucracy effectively. Broder contents that "With a single six-year term for president, the bureaucracy would respond even less to executive direction and become even more dependent upon its permanent patrons in Congress."[47]

3. The media: What the president does is news and thus is the subject of scrutiny and interpretation by the press corps. Conflict is inevitable, as is fitting in a politically competitive environment. Critics of a single six-year term argue that limiting the president's term to six years will not remove media criticism, and making the presidency weaker will make it harder for the president to win media praise.

4. Interest groups: An active president needs interest groups as much as

interest groups need the president. There is no special unbiased means for determining what is in the public interest. The First Amendment preserves the right "to petition the government," but beyond that there is the continuing need for information about public problems and the effectiveness of programs designed to solve public problems. The opponents of a single term contend that a rarefied, nonpolitical process of decision making is neither realistic nor desirable.

5. The political party: Perhaps no expectations, it is argued, are as illusory as those associated with the political party and the single term. What is proposed in connection with the nonpartisan president is a headless political party. In 1960 Clinton Rossiter argued that a second-term president who tried to abdicate the party role "would be worse than a lame duck: he would be a dead one. . . . While the vision of the nonpartisan President will always beckon us, it is fated to remain no more than a vision."[48] The Twenty-second Amendment and other antiparty reforms have taken their toll, however, and the nonpartisan president is no longer a vision. The single-term reform would be another move against the party system, with greater loss of party discipline and leadership.

6. The public: Representing the general public is a continuous process involving political contacts with interest groups, Congress, the media, national party leaders, state and local leaders, and the agencies. There is no magic, it is argued, by means of which a single term will transform an elected president into some kind of "seer" of the public interest. But if a president pretends to that role without maintaining communication with the groups named, what checks are available short of impeachment? A six-year term may encourage a president to ignore public opinion and the public interest in the daily administration of his office. A president elected for six years who is unresponsive may do much damage to the general public before a corrective can be implemented.

Additional reasons for opposition. Opponents of the single term do not find expectations of proponents regarding the effect of office on the president and his family to be relevant arguments for change. The office is demanding, but the Constitution is not the proper vehicle for decisions on the capacity of all persons to hold it. That seeking reelection is in some way degrading is a sentiment so antidemocratic as to be unacceptable in the present debate. And, whereas it is regrettable that family privacy is sacrificed in the White House, there are repairs to that problem short of a constitutional amendment.

LIMITING HOUSE AND SENATE TENURE

A subtle but important shift has occurred in the rationale for reforming congressional terms. As has been noted, little attention was paid historically to changing the six-year term for senators, but the four-year term proposal for House members was recommended so that legislators who were becoming more professional would not have to run every second year. The recent discovery that biennial elections do not necessarily result in high turnover of membership appears to have spawned a different type of reform—that of limiting the number of terms that can be served (whether these terms are set at two, three, or four years). The reform would be extended to the Senate as well, although turnover in recent years has been consistently higher among those standing for reelection there than in the House. As is the case with presidential term limitation, proponents and opponents of change have contrasting theories about the most effective composition of a legislature, which leads to contrasting expectations regarding the consequences of limitation. Thus, each section below will be organized to treat (1) the general theory of politics which supports each view, (2) the estimates of an acceptable period of service, and (3) the expectations of benefits to be realized.[49]

Views of Supporters of Limited Tenure. The principal arguments of proponents will be discussed, together with advantages accruing in the relationships outside Congress and within Congress itself.

Principal arguments of proponents. The frequency of House elections was judged by Hamilton or Madison, writing in *The Federalist*, to be sufficient to provide "an immediate dependence on, and an intimate sympathy with, the people."

> Frequent elections are unquestionably the only policy by which this dependence and sympathy can be effectually secured. But what particular degree of frequency may be absolutely necessary for the purpose, does not appear to be susceptible of any precise calculation.[50]

Turning to experience as a guide, Hamilton or Madison concluded that "biennial elections will be as useful to the affairs of the public, as we have seen that they will be safe to the liberty of the people."[51] The longer Senate term was justified on the basis of a need for a "legislative department, which, having sufficient permanency to provide for such objects as require a continued attention, and a train of measures, may be justly and effectually answerable for the attainment of those objects."[52]

The authors of *The Federalist* addressed concerns that the Senate might "transform itself, by gradual usurpation, into an independent and aristocratic body," and satisfied themselves that sufficient checks were provided to prevent bad effects in the unlikely event that "such a revolution should ever happen."[53]

The problems of too much continuity were never treated directly and, as has been noted earlier, they did not seriously arise during the nineteenth century because of the relatively high turnover in Congress. In recent years, however, there has been increasing concern with what seem to some to be interminable lengths of tenure in office accompanied by "abuses of arrogance and empire."[54]

Critics of indefinite tenure are often linked to the Jacksonian view of the corrupting nature of power and the need for frequent rotation in office, as applied to the president. Senator Dennis DeConcini (D-Ariz.), principal sponsor of limiting total tenure summarizes his general theory as follows:

> On a more philosophical level, I am deeply committed to the concept of the citizen-legislator. An enlarged pool of political candidates would

> certainly generate a wealth of new ideas. The growth of the professional legislator on the other hand is frightening, for it is yet another step away from the democratic ideal, leading toward rigid, unrepresentative institutions.[55]

This statement is revealing of a perspective repeated in one form or another by most advocates of limiting tenure in office. It is not enough to have frequent elections to ensure either a citizen-based legislature or true representation. For DeConcini, the authors of *The Federalist* are wrong: "dependence" and "sympathy" *cannot* be "effectually secured" by frequent elections alone. Continuity may still result from frequent elections, and continuity can have a number of unfavorable effects, for example, lack of contact with the people, failure to develop new ideas, increased perquisites that maintain an incumbent in office, alliances with other branches of government, the desire for reelection merely to maintain a career, a growing cynicism, and distrust by the public.

Senator John C. Danforth (R-Mo.) argues that the congressman who serves for life is not "of the people." He contends that "the growth and cost of government has skyrocketed as congressmen say anything, do anything, and spend anything to get themselves reelected." In his view much of the power of the federal government—power obtained at the expense of the states—can be traced to the amount of time senators and representatives spend in Washington. He claims that by forcing turnover in Congress we may be able to decentralize power from Washington.[56]

The argument for limiting terms to force greater turnover finds support in the benefits of office which enable incumbents to be reelected with such regularity—$610,000 per member of Congress per year by one estimate.[57]

Representative Elwood Hillis (R-Ind.) argues that terms should be limited to help disperse among more members of Congress the awesome power gained by some legislators through seniority and committee chairmanships. He asks, "Can equal representation be served when one Senator or Congressman holds substantially more power and influence than any other member?"[58]

In summary, many support a congressional tenure limitation from a desire for a citizen-based or amateur-based legislature. Professionalism is not accepted as a virtue in this setting. Indeed, it appears that the advocates of term limitation make distinctions among direct democracy, representative democracy, and professional or technocratic democracy. The first is acknowledged to be an impossible achievement at the national level. The last is judged to have emerged in Congress with the growth of incumbency advantage complemented by staff increases and other perquisites. It is this development toward professional democracy that should be curbed, they argue—at least as it is evidenced in Congress. This leaves representative democracy as the goal to be achieved, or recaptured. "What is sought here . . . is greater responsiveness and greater representativeness," according to Senator DeConcini. What is sought further is a less complex, a more comprehensible, legislature, in which citizens can operate effectively without disadvantage caused by lack of longevity. As Robert L. Riebow, director of government sales for Best Foods, stated at a business symposium on the issue:

It is necessary to diminish the sustained influence of the legislative demigods. Authentic servants of the people can continue their contributions outside government. No state or congressional district is so short of talent that it cannot replace a legislator with another equally as effective.[59]

This concept of legislative service as within the capacity of many, if not all, intelligent citizens seems to be at the heart of the advocate's philosophical position.

If a cap on legislative service is necessary, the question that naturally arises is: How long should legislators be permitted to serve? Most responses call for twelve years for each house—six two-year, four three-year, or three four-year terms for representatives, and two six-year terms for senators. Typically, no cap is placed on service in both institutions, nor is state or local legislative service mentioned.[60]

It is interesting to note that little or no analysis or reasoning is offered for twelve years as a solution to the problems of incumbency. The six-year term for the president is justified as a reasonable length of time for adjusting to the position and for having a subsequent impact on public policy. There does not appear to be a similar rationale for twelve years in the House or the Senate. In the Senate Subcommittee on the Constitution's hearings on congressional tenure, those members supporting change argued that the more important matter was tenure limitation as a principle, not the number of years.[61] Thus, the number of years included in most proposals appears to be relatively arbitrary—possibly being set for Senate terms first, since the six-year term provides fewer options for a limit (for example, six, twelve, eighteen, or twenty-four years total service), and then being matched in the House. However it has been set, the available commentaries do not include policy or representational justifications for the twelve-year limit.

The set of expectations associated with limiting congressional tenure is less elaborate than is the case with presidential tenure limitations. The perceived benefits are seen as a consequence of reducing the evils associated with excessively long tenure rather than with the temptations of reelection. The latter is involved, of course, but reelection is judged to be a "good," in moderation. It is only when reelection occurs repeatedly that it becomes a vice. The expected benefits, therefore, can be divided into those realized in the outside relationships of members of Congress and those realized within the two houses.

Benefits in outside relationships. The advantages of term limitations for senators' and representatives' relationships outside Congress are seen to be the following:

1. States and districts: States and districts will be better represented because of higher turnover and greater competition. Senators and representatives will be less likely to succumb to "Potomac Fever," and therefore will be more attentive to major public problems in their home areas. At the same time, less time will be spent on performing small favors for constituents since reelection will not be the prime goal of the citizen-legislators.

2. Special interests: Members who do not expect to remain in Congress for a

long period of time will not need heavy support, will be less beholden to special interests, and will be more inclined to consider the public interest. Limited tenure will have the effect of making legislative service avocational and thus concentrated on broader issues. Therefore, special interests will be less able to buy influence through campaign contributions or other favors.

3. Cozy triangles: Members will be less inclined to join the "cozy triangles" of bureaucrats and lobbyists that characterize so much of policy making. They will be independent of these relatively invisible power centers and thus will be better able to check their influence.

4. Relative power of the president and Congress: Some students of public affairs feel that the system of checks and balances provided in the Constitution is wise, but that events of recent years, including the imposition of a limit on presidential tenure, have altered the balance or distribution of power between the executive and legislative branches. In their view, if presidential power is curtailed through a limit on tenure then as a corollary congressional power should be similarly limited.

Benefits within the Congress. Typically, many of those favoring limited congressional terms are most concerned about the internal operations of the House and Senate. The advantages are judged to be those discussed immediately below.

1. Infusion of new ideas: Once challengers recognize that the incumbent's advantage is nullified, the channels which bring fresh ideas and new approaches to pressing social problems will indeed be opened.[62] The change will, therefore, truly bring a new legislature into being—one that is not tied to the stale and tired programs of the past.

2. Distribution of power: Even with recent changes in the seniority system, longevity continues to be a source of power within Congress. Limiting tenure, it is claimed, is the ultimate solution to this unfair distribution of power.

3. Reduced costs of running Congress: Many of the perquisites of office are designed to reelect incumbents. With reduced incentive to be reelected, members will be in a position to conduct an objective review of the need for these perquisites, including the enormous staff assistance that has developed on Capitol Hill in recent years.

4. Concentration on the major issues: Freed from concern for perpetuating themselves in office indefinitely, legislators will concentrate on broad, cross-cutting issues. Under the present circumstances Congress is too much involved with incremental changes in existing programs, and the larger issues are frequently ignored. Citizen-legislators will not have so great a stake in the present way of doing things.

Views of Opponents of Limited Tenure. The chief arguments of opponents are discussed, and rebuttals are given to the advantages claimed for limited tenure.

The principal thrust of opposition. The general theory that forms the basis for the views of those opposing limited congressional tenure is not unlike that of those opposing limited presidential tenure. That is, the opponents see great virtue in elections as the principal corrective to the problems of Congress. Thomas E. Mann, assistant director of the American Political Science Association and codirector of the Congress Project, American Enterprise Institute, stated the case in his testimony against the proposed limitations:

> The first argument against the amendment is that it really is an infringement on individual liberties, both the liberties of the voters and office holders. Moreover it is essentially antidemocratic. It just does not trust the electorate to decide for itself whether an individual should be returned to office or not. In fact, it substitutes an arbitrary rule for the collective judgment of citizens in this country.[63]

This is not to say that the opponents do not recognize problems associated with incumbency advantage, or that they are opposed to turnover. Rather, they emphasize the importance of identifying the precise problems associated with incumbency—for example, excessive perquisites, competitive advantage, seniority—and of solving those problems rather than making constitutional adjustments. On this point Austin Ranney, past president of the American Political Science Association and codirector of Political and Social Processes Studies of the American Enterprise Institute, testified as follows:

> If one accepts that principle, i.e., "If it ain't broke, don't fix it," then . . . there is a real burden of proof on the people who want to change the system . . . to show . . . a major evil that exists in letting senators and representatives be elected and reelected as many times as the voters in their districts and States are willing to do so. The advocates also must show that the clear evil can be remedied only by depriving people of their right freely to elect and reelect their senators and representatives as long as they want to.[64]

Perhaps the principal difference between the proponents and opponents of limited tenure can best be summarized in terms of the contrasting estimates of gains and losses. The proponents believe more is to be gained by forcing turnover than will be lost by removing experienced legislators. The opponents believe that more is to be gained by permitting reelection than will be lost by lengthy incumbency. But the opponents also emphasize the importance of politics generally. As Norman Ornstein, associate professor of political science, Catholic University of America, and fellow at the Center for Advanced Studies in Behaviorial Science, Stanford University, testified, "We think public service through the electoral mechanism is something to be exalted and not something to be denigrated."[65]

The opponents to term limitation do not have a reaction to the appropriate length of service, since they disagree with establishing any limit at all. But one opponent, Thomas E. Mann, raises the fundamental point that the incumbency factor may not be as important as it is often considered to be:

> One curious thing is that the longer incumbents stay in office the more

vulnerable they become. It turns out, in fact, that one can look at the House and see the probability of reelection . . . is highest in mid-career—second term, third term, and fourth term—but when members start 11 terms, or 12 terms, or 14 terms, the probability of losing increases.[66]

Mann also questions the conclusion that incumbency results in unresponsiveness. "On the contrary, the members are now more than ever likely to represent their constituents' interests at all stages of the legislative process."[67]

In view of their objection to the observations and conclusions of the proponents, it is not surprising that the opponents react negatively to the set of expectations regarding the effects of term limitation outside and inside the Congress.

Rebuttal to claims of benefits in outside relationships. 1. State and district: Critics claim that proponents have inconsistent expectations. On one hand they expect that legislators with limited terms will be better representatives of the people and will be less likely to establish permanent residence in Washington. On the other hand they claim that members will not be "errand boys" performing minor favors for constituents. In fact, there is little evidence that the members are not now representing their states and districts well, or that tenure limitation will actually produce an improved quality of representation. In fact, members will run for reelection within the total period of service permitted, and they can be expected to behave just as members of Congress now do.

2. Special interests: Critics argue that representatives will be more, rather than less, closely tied to special interests. They must still be elected, though possibly for fewer terms on the average. And their presumed avocational interests may, in fact, be no more than special attention to a group with which they are identified in their private occupation. This has not been an uncommon phenomenon at the state level—for example, lawyers, realtors, and businessmen take time out to run for the legislature to further their private interests. Career legislators, on the other hand, may be better insulated from special interests, particularly if these legislators are provided with professional staffs.

3. Cozy triangles: It does not necessarily follow that members with limited terms will not participate actively in the policy networks that have come to characterize government decision making. They may find such arrangements highly accommodating to those special interests they potentially represent. Or, if some do not participate, these centers of power may be expected to operate without direct involvement of those members of Congress. In any event, the longevity and the experience of members of Congress have been important countering forces to an entrenched bureaucracy. As Austin Ranney has stated, "I wonder how we are going to control that [bureaucracy] with the Congress, . . . whose members [not only] have limited service before them but . . . become lame ducks when they are elected to their last elective term."[68]

Rebuttal to claims of benefits for Congress. 1. Infusion of new ideas: It is impossible to debate this issue without establishing a measure of the flow of new ideas into Congress as it is presently constituted and without determining the means that might develop with tenure limitations to ensure an even greater flow. Without these indicators, a case can be made either way, simply on the basis of the hunches of those involved in the debate.

2. Distribution of power: Limiting tenure will not automatically distribute power to new members of Congress. Seniority within the new constraints may well be the means of distributing power internally. Or, what is more important, congressional power itself may decline in relation to the president and the bureaucracy. Finally, unless the burgeoning legislative staff is reduced or otherwise curbed, temporary legislators may lose power to permanent Hill bureaucrats who are substantially less accountable to the voters.

3. Reduced costs of running Congress: Many of the perquisites of office are necessary so that representatives and senators can represent more heavily populated districts and states (the House has not been expanded since 1912 when the average population per district was 211,000; today it is approximately 500,000) and can legislate on increasingly complex issues. Amateur legislators may require more, not fewer, perquisites (such as staff), thus raising the cost of Congress. Much may depend on whether Congress loses power to the other branches of government as a consequence of reform. A rubber-stamp legislature does not require many perquisites.

4. Concentration on the major issues: This claimed advantage is subject to the same rebuttal as that concerning the infusion of new ideas. Major cross-cutting issues are now treated in every session of Congress. Why more such issues would be taken up by a legislature whose members can only run for a limited number of terms is not clear and is certainly not evident from the assertions made by the proponents of change.

Table 1
SEQUENCE OF ACTION ON PRESIDENTIAL LENGTH OF TERM AND SUCCESSION AT THE CONSTITUTIONAL CONVENTION, 1787

Date	Action Taken
May 29	Randolph introduced Virginia Plan. National executive chosen by the legislature; length of tenure left blank; not eligible for reelection.
	Pinckney introduced plan. Length of presidential term unspecified but president eligible for reelection.
June 1	Debate held in the Committee of the Whole on presidential term. Set at 7 years by a vote of 5 to 4, with one delegation divided. (New York, New Jersey, Pennsylvania, Delaware, and Virginia in favor; Connecticut, North Carolina, South Carolina, and Georgia opposed; Massachusetts divided.)
June 2	Further debate held on selection of president. Ineligibility for second term voted 7 to 2, with one delegation divided. (Massachusetts, New York,

Date	Action Taken
	Delaware, Maryland, Virginia, North Carolina, and South Carolina in favor; Connecticut and Georgia opposed; Pennsylvania divided.)
June 13	Report of the Committee of the Whole completed (including one 7-year term for president—elected by the legislature and not eligible for reelection).
June 15	Paterson introduced New Jersey Plan; federal executive chosen by Congress; length of term left blank; not eligible for reelection.
	Hamilton introduced plan; governor to be elected and serve during good behavior.
June 19	Report of the Committee of the Whole presented to the Convention; debate begun.
July 17	Houston moved to strike the clause "to be ineligible a second time." Approved by a vote of 6 to 4. (Massachusetts, Connecticut, New Jersey, Pennsylvania, Maryland, and Georgia in favor; Delaware, Virginia, North Carolina, and South Carolina opposed.)
	McClurg moved to strike "7 years" and insert "during good behavior." Defeated by a vote of 6 to 4. (New Jersey, Pennsylvania, Delaware, and Virginia in favor; Massachusetts, Connecticut, Maryland, North Carolina, South Carolina, and Georgia opposed.)
July 19	Martin moved to reinstate ineligibility for a second term. Defeated by a vote of 8 to 2. (North Carolina and South Carolina in favor; Massachusetts, Connecticut, New Jersey, Pennsylvania, Delaware, Maryland, Virginia, and Georgia opposed.)
	Seven-year term put to the convention. Defeated by a vote of 3 to 5, with two delegations divided. (Connecticut, South Carolina, and Georgia in favor; New Jersey, Pennsylvania, Delaware, Maryland, and Virginia opposed; Massachusetts and North Carolina divided.)
	Ellsworth proposed 6-year terms. Approved by a vote of 9 to 1. (Massachusetts, Connecticut, New Jersey, Pennsylvania, Maryland, Virginia, North Carolina, South Carolina, and Georgia in favor; Delaware opposed.)
July 24	Martin and Gerry moved to reinstate ineligibility for a second term. Various term lengths proposed: Martin, 11 years; Gerry, 15 years; King, 20 years; Davie, 8 years. Wilson moved that consideration of all proposals be postponed—first defeated, then approved when reintroduced by King.
July 25	Pinckney moved that "no person shall serve in the executive more than 6 years in 12." Defeated by a vote of 5 to 6. (New Hampshire, Massachusetts, North Carolina, South Carolina, and Georgia in favor; Connecticut, New Jersey, Pennsylvania, Delaware, Maryland, and Virginia opposed.)
July 26	Original language reintroduced; a 7-year term; ineligible for reelection. Approved by a vote of 6 to 3, with one delegation divided. (New Hampshire, Connecticut, New Jersey, North Carolina, South Carolina, and Georgia in favor; Pennsylvania, Delaware, and Maryland opposed; Massachusetts divided.)
August 6	Report of the Committee on Detail recommended a single 7-year term.

Date	Action Taken
August 31	Several postponed parts of the Constitution referred to a Committee of Eleven (Gilman, King, Sherman, Brearly, Gouverneur Morris, Dickinson, Carroll, Madison, Williamson, Butler, and Baldwin).
September 4	Committee of Eleven recommended a 4-year term for the president, with no restriction on reelection.
September 6	Spaight and Williamson moved to change from 4- to 7-year term. Defeated by a vote of 8 to 3. (New Hampshire, Virginia, and North Carolina in favor; Massachusetts, Connecticut, New Jersey, Pennsylvania, Delaware, Maryland, South Carolina, and Georgia opposed.)
	Spaight and Williamson moved to change from 4- to 6-year term. Defeated by a vote of 9 to 2. (North Carolina and South Carolina in favor; New Hampshire, Massachusetts, Connecticut, New Jersey, Pennsylvania, Delaware, Maryland, Virginia, and Georgia opposed.)
September 8	All resolutions referred to Committee on Revision (Johnson, Hamilton, Gouverneur Morris, Madison, and King).
September 12	Report of Committee on Revision made (including a 4-year term for the president).
September 15	Constitution as amended agreed to (including a 4-year term for the president).

Source: Compiled from Charles C. Tansill, ed., *Documents Illustrative of the Formation of the Union of the American States* (Washington, D.C.: Government Printing Office, 1927), James Madison, "Debates in The Federal Convention of 1787," in *Documents Illustrative of the Formation of The Union of The American States* (Washington, D.C.: Government Printing Office, 1927), pp. 109–745; and Paul Dwyer, *Presidential Tenure; A History and Examination of the President's Term of Office,* (Washington, D.C.: Congressional Research Service, Library of Congress, December 31, 1974), pp. 1–10.

Table 2
REPRESENTATIVE RESOLUTIONS TO LENGTHEN AND/OR LIMIT PRESIDENTIAL AND/OR CONGRESSIONAL TERMS OR TENURE, 96TH CONGRESS, 1ST SESSION

Resolution	President	House	Senate	Other Provisions
H.J. Res. 22	—	4-yr. terms, staggered elections, 3-term limit	6-yr. terms, 2-term limit	Representative must resign to run for Senate
H.J. Res. 50	6-yr. term, 2-term limit, 15-yr. limit	3-yr. terms, 12-yr. limit	6-yr. terms, 12-yr. limit	½ of senators elected every third yr.; 18 yr. limit on combined House-Senate service

Resolution	President	House	Senate	Other Provisions
H.J. Res. 65	—	4-yr. terms, off-year elections	—	Representative must resign to run for Senate
H.J. Res. 114	—	Service limited to 6 consecutive Congresses—House and Senate		Sitting senators may serve out term
H.J. Res. 160	6-yr. term, 9-yr. limit	2-yr. terms, 13-yr. limit	6-yr. terms, 15-yr. limit	15-yr. limit for judges of Supreme Ct. and inferior cts.
H.J. Res. 169	—	2-yr. terms, 9-term limit	6-yr. terms, 3-term limit	—
H.J. Res. 170 H.J. Res. 179	—	4-yr. terms, staggered elections, 3-term limit, 14-yr. limit	6-yr. terms, 2-term limit, 15-yr. limit	—
H.J. Res. 182	6-yr. term, 9-yr. limit	4-yr. terms, 3-term limit, 14-yr. limit	6-yr. terms, 2-term limit, 15-yr. limit	Provisions not applicable to sitting officials at time of ratification
H.J. Res. 186	6-yr. term, 1-term limit	3-yr. terms, 5-term limit	6-yr. terms, 3-term limit	Age limit of 75 yrs.
H.J. Res. 315	—	10-yr. limit in any 12-yr. period	12-yr. limit in any 14-yr. period	—
H.J. Res. 334	—	4-yr. terms, 12-yr. limit	12-yr. limit	Person who attains age of 70 during term of office may be elected president, vice president, senator, or representative

Resolution	President	House	Senate	Other Provisions
H.J. Res. 368	—	8-yr. limit	4-yr. terms, 8-yr. limit	—
H.J. Res. 377	6-yr. term, 1-term limit, vice-president succeeding to presidency limited to 9 years	—	—	—
S.J. Res. 25	—	2-yr. terms, 6-term limit	6-yr. terms, 2-term limit	Elections prior to ratification not taken into account
S.J. Res. 27	—	2-yr. terms, 7-term limit, 15-yr. limit	6-yr. terms, 2-term limit, 14-yr. limit	Elections prior to ratification not taken into account
S.J. Res. 34	—	4-yr. terms, elected w/president	—	Representative must resign to run for Senate
S.J. Res. 103	6-yr. term, 1 term limit, vice-president succeeding to presidency limited to 8 years	—	—	—

Source: Compiled from resolutions supplied by U.S. Senate, Committee on the Judiciary.

NOTES TO TEXT

[1] Interview with President Jimmy Carter, UPI Newspaper Advisory Board, April 27, 1979.

[2] Both quotations from James Madison, "Debates in the Federal Convention of 1787," in *Documents Illustrative of the Formation of the Union of the American States*, ed. Charles C. Tansill (Washington, D.C.: Government Printing Office, 1927), p. 396. For good summary analyses of the debates on this topic, see Joseph F. Kallenbach, "Constitutional Limitations on Reeligibility of National and State Chief Executives," *American Political Science Review*, vol. 46 (June 1952), pp. 438–454; Max Farrand, "Election and Term of the President," *Yale Review*, vol. 2 (April 1913), pp. 510–520; and John W. Perrin, "Presidential Tenure and Reeligibility," *Political Science Quarterly*, vol. 29 (September 1914), pp. 423–437.

[3] Madison, "Debates," p. 397.

[4] Ibid., p. 663.

[5] Ibid., p. 678.

[6] In fact, the issue was the subject of considerable debate in the state ratifying conventions. Three state conventions adopted recommendations that Congress should submit an amendment to the states limiting presidential tenure. See Kallenbach, "Constitutional Limitations," p. 440.

[7] James Thomas Flexner, *Washington: The Indispensable Man* (Boston: Little, Brown and Company, 1974), p. 347.

[8] Quoted in Paul Dwyer, *Presidential Tenure: A History and Examination of the President's Term of Office* (Washington, D.C.: Congressional Research Service, Library of Congress, December 31, 1974), p. 12. See also Stefan Lorant, *The Presidency* (New York: The Macmillan Company, 1952), p. 326. The Dwyer study was of great value in the preparation of this analysis—both for the material presented and for the bibliography.

[9] Grant sought to run again in 1880, however, without success. See Lorant, *The Presidency*, p. 340, and Edward S. Corwin, *The President: Office and Powers* (New York: New York University Press, 1957), p. 35.

[10] Corwin, *The President*, p. 36.

[11] Ibid.

[12] Congressional Quarterly, Inc., *Congress and the Nation*, vol. 1 (Washington, D.C.: Congressional Quarterly, Inc., 1965), p. 1434.

[13] For a review of the debate on the amendment, see Kallenbach, "Constitutional Limitations"; Perrin, "Presidential Tenure"; and Everett S. Brown, "The Term of Office of the President," *American Political Science Review*, vol. 41 (June 1947), pp. 447–452.

[14] Edmund Cody Burnett, *The Continental Congress* (New York: W. W. Norton & Company, 1964), p. 250.

[15] Ibid., p. 605.

[16] Ibid.

[17] Ibid., pp. 605–606.

[18] Madison, "Debates," pp. 192–193.

[19] Ibid., p. 192.

[20] Both quotations from ibid., p. 256.

[21] Ibid., pp. 280–281.

[22] Madison and Sherman quotations from ibid., p. 281.

[23] H. Douglas Price, "The Congressional Career—Then and Now," in *Congressional Behavior*, ed. Nelson W. Polsby (New York: Random House, 1971), p. 16.

[24] For a review of these efforts, see Sula P. Richardson, *Term of Office for Members of the U.S. House of Representatives: A History and Select Bibliography* (Washington, D.C.: Congressional Research Service, Library of Congress, April 24, 1978), pp. 4–14. See also Charles O. Jones, *Every Second Year* (Washington, D.C.: Brookings Institution, 1967), Ch. 2.

[25] The polls mentioned in this paragraph are summarized in Jones, *Every Second Year*, pp. 22–24. Representative Chelf reported on his poll in U.S. Congress, House of Representatives, Subcommittee No. 5 of the Committee on the Judiciary, *Hearings on Congressional Tenure of Office*, 89th Congress, 1st and 2nd sessions, 1965-1966, p. 19.

[26] Jones, *Every Second Year*, pp. 105–112.

[27] Taken from the compilation in Foundation for the Study of Presidential and Congressional Terms, "Constitutional Background and Legislative History of Proposals to Limit Years of Congressional Service," Washington, D.C., 1979. (Mimeographed.)

[28] There are numerous sources for the arguments reflected here. Many of the sources are repetitive. Those relied on here include: Dwyer, *Presidential Tenure;* Foundation for the Study of Presidential and Congressional Terms, "Constitutional Background and Legislative History of Proposals to Limit Presidential Service"; "Proposals to Establish a Single Six-Year Presidential Term," *Congressional Digest*, vol. 51 (March 1972), pp. 68–96; Jack Valenti, "The Case for a Six-Year Presidency," *Saturday Review*, vol. 51 (August 3, 1968), p. 13; George E. Reedy, *The Twilight of the Presidency* (New York: World Publishing Company, 1979), pp. 137–147; Morris K. Udall, "A Six-Year Presidency?" *The Progressive*, vol. 38 (June 1974), pp. 19–20; William G. Carleton, "A Six-Year Term for the President?" *South Atlantic Quarterly*, vol. 71 (Spring 1972), pp. 165–176; and *The Federalist* (New York: Random House, Modern Library, 1937), No. 72, pp. 468–474. Dwyer includes an extensive bibliography in his paper, pp. 57–66.

[29] Quoted in Dwyer, *Presidential Tenure*, p. 37.

[30] Milton S. Eisenhower, "Why We Should Limit Congressional Terms," *Washington Post*, April 18, 1978, p. A-19.

[31] Quoted in Leonard D. White, *The Jacksonians* (New York: The Macmillan Company, 1954), p. 318.

[32] Quoted in David S. Broder, "A Frail Amendment," *Washington Post,* February 11, 1979, p. L-7.

[33] Quoted in Dwyer, *Presidential Tenure,* p. 47.

[34] Kallenbach, "Constitutional Limitations," pp. 451–454, does provide analysis of experience at the state level. One conclusion is that the executive loses effectiveness as a legislative leader "as the time for his enforced retirement nears."

[35] Early supporters of the single six-year term argued that it would alleviate the patronage problem of the president (for example, Grover Cleveland—see Dwyer, *Presidential Tenure,* p. 39). President Kennedy later observed, however, that patronage is not a factor.

[36] President Carter has stated: "No matter what I do as president now, where I am really trying to ignore politics and stay away from any sort of campaign plans and so forth, a lot of the things I do are colored through the news media and in the minds of the American people by [the question] 'Is this a campaign ploy or is it genuinely done . . . in the best interest of our country without any sort of personal advantage involved?'" "Carter Now Favors Single 6-Year Term," *Washington Star,* April 29, 1979, p. A-3.

[37] Quoted in Dwyer, *Presidential Tenure,* p. 45.

[38] Quoted in Broder, "A Frail Amendment."

[39] *The Federalist,* No. 72, pp. 470–473.

[40] Ibid., pp. 469–470.

[41] See Charles Bartlett, "That Six-Year Term," *Washington Star,* May 2, 1979, p. A-19.

[42] Quoted in Dwyer, *Presidential Tenure,* p. 43, from Testimony of President Harry S. Truman before the U.S. Senate Subcommittee on Constitutional Amendments of the Committee on the Judiciary, *Hearings on Presidential Tenure,* 86th Congress, 1st Session, 1959.

[43] Broder, "A Frail Amendment."

[44] Reedy, *Twilight of the Presidency,* p. 139.

[45] Ibid., 138–139.

[46] Broder, "A Frail Amendment."

[47] Ibid.

[48] Clinton Rossiter, *The American Presidency* (New York: Harcourt Brace & World, 1960), p. 235.

[49] As is the case with presidential term limitation, a great many sources are available on this topic. The sample drawn on here includes: U.S. Congress, Senate, Subcommittee on the Constitution of the Committee on the Judiciary, *Hearings on Congressional Tenure,* 95th Congress, 2nd session (1978); Richardson, "Term of Office"; Foundation for the Study of Presidential and Congressional Terms, "Constitutional Background and Legislative History of Proposals to Limit Years of Congressional Service"; Jones, *Every Second Year;* Milton

S. Eisenhower, "Why We Should Limit Congressional Terms," "Congressional Term Limits Get More Public Support Still Unpopular on Hill," *Congressional Quarterly Weekly Report,* vol. 36 (February 25, 1978) pp. 533–534; "12 Years in Washington Is Time Enough," *Nation's Business,* vol. 66 (August 1978), pp. 18–21; and *The Federalist.*

[50] *The Federalist,* No. 52, p. 343.

[51] Ibid., No. 53, p. 353.

[52] Ibid., No. 64, p. 409.

[53] Ibid., p. 416.

[54] "Limiting Terms," *Indianapolis News,* February 10, 1979, editorial.

[55] Senate Subcommittee on the Constitution, *Congressional Tenure,* p. 5.

[56] Quoted in "Should Congressional Terms be Limited to 12 Years?" *American Legion Magazine,* vol. 107 (March 1979), p. 10; John C. Danforth, "Limiting Congressional Tenure," *Congressional Record,* vol. 125 (January 24, 1979), p. S 595.

[57] Monty Hoyt, "$610,000: Annual Cost per Member of Congress," *Christian Science Monitor,* January 29, 1975.

[58] Elwood Hillis, "Limitation on Terms for Members of Congress," *Congressional Record,* vol. 124 (October 14, 1978), pp. E 5544–E 5546.

[59] Quoted in "12 Years in Washington Is Time Enough," p. 18.

[60] One proposal, H.J. Res. 50, by Hillis, would limit service in the two houses to eighteen years.

[61] See Senate Subcommittee on the Constitution, *Congressional Tenure,* p. 83.

[62] Ibid., p. 5.

[63] Ibid., p. 41.

[64] Ibid., p. 43.

[65] Ibid., p. 44.

[66] Ibid., p. 46. See also Robert S. Erikson, "Is There Such a Thing as a Safe Seat?" *Polity,* vol. 8 (Summer 1976), pp. 57–66.

[67] Thomas E. Mann, *Unsafe at Any Margin* (Washington, D.C.: American Enterprise Institute, 1978), p. 105.

[68] Senate Subcommittee on the Constitution, *Congressional Tenure,* p. 48.

WIDENER UNIVERSITY-WOLFGRAM LIBRARY
CIR   JK550.A43
Limiting presidential and congressional
DISCARD
3 3182 00180 0199

JK
550   .A43   161631